Selling Contracting Services – 101

William (Bill) C. McElroy

ISBN 9781693892578

Preface:

This book was written in 2011 as a construction industry-training manual. It is now updated to 2019 and although it is aimed at those that wish to sell construction services, it is applicable to anyone that makes a living 'selling' a product or service as the tips, warnings, and procedural techniques are basically the same.

Author:

The author, now retired, in his prime was a building designer, contractor, and builder. He has published construction books and articles for Prentice Hall, Craftsman Book Company, Family Handyman Magazine; taught several construction courses at B.O.C.E.S. in Goshen, New York, and has served as an 'Expert Witness' in court case contractor/client disputes.

Table of Contents:

Introduction:

You may be new to the industry or you may have spent years in school, or as an apprentice, or as an individual doing contracting work and now it is time to expand and show off your talents, but to whom and where?

There are three basic parts to selling a job, the first is the *marketing and advertising*, then comes the *contact and selling*, followed by the doing and follow-up *marketing and advertising*. Yes, it is a loop that can be self-feeding, if you understand the principles behind advertising and salesmanship. This informative guide to your success is designed to help you help yourself to more and better sales, and most importantly, profitable sales.

Dedicated to:

Those professionals that have taken the time and energy to expand their knowledge and thus, provide good products and services to the communities that they serve.

Advertising & Selling Your Services:

Why Do I Have to Learn How to Sell?

The simple answer is that if you do not, you will not have a company that makes a living for you and yours. The long answer is that it will improve the bottom line and help you grow your contracting business, even if you want to remain a one-person business, or if you have aspirations to take over the construction world. Many people are very talented, and you as a reader of this text probably are too; you may be an excellent plumber, or electrician, or mason, etc. but your talent is no good to anyone, if no one knows about it. Advertising is the passing on of the information that you are the 'expert', that you are 'in business', that you are 'available' for hire, and that you are 'professional'.

What does advertising have to do with selling, and what is the difference? The advertising brings the client to your door, a door in which they have to be persuaded to enter. The selling brings you to their door, a door that they open for you and to which you are invited.

3

What Can I Gain From Learning How to Sell My Services?

You can learn to 'close' a sale, and that is the name of the game. Later in this guide you will see examples of Overcoming Objections, turning a NO SALE into a sale, and the art of 'Closing' the deal. These are people skills that require knowledge of what people want, are thinking, and will pay for with his or her hard-earned dollars. Just because you are offering a product or service, and you may be the sole provider or the local expert, it does not mean that you can just sit back and expect people to come to you and offer you their dollars; you have to earn those dollars and the first step in earning those dollars is getting the job.

What Media Should I Use?

The media for advertising your construction or contracting services depends on several local factors, including the availability of media. Many areas of the country do not have a local newspaper, or local radio station, or local Chamber of Commerce, and therefore these media are not available to you. The best media is that media where you find your competition or other contractors doing their advertising, for they have 'tested the waters' and found that they get responses for their advertising investments.

There are all sorts of media for advertising and each will be covered in this advertising and salesmanship guide; it is up to you to determine what works for you, and that will be by trial and error.

How Much Will It Cost Me?

How much will it cost you to not advertise? If you have invested in trade schooling, equipment, a brick and mortar building, employees, and such, and there are no jobs available for which to earn money to pay for these items, then not advertising gets very expensive.

Unfortunately, too many businesses cut back during hard times, and one of the first items most cut is the advertising budget, the one item that he or she should be increasing by spending more.

So, what is the cost of advertising, it cost nothing, if it is effective and brings in clients and profitable jobs. It can cost considerably, if not aimed at the proper market and properly presented. Usually, there is a balance between the two, and most accountants will suggest about 4% to 8% of your Gross Earnings should go to advertising. Thus if you are earning $200 per day, you should be spending $8 to $16 per day on advertising, and this expenditure is included in your hourly rates, thus an eight hour day will have $1.00 to $2.00 per hour of advertising cost.

Can I Afford This?

You can, and you must, if you want to stay in business. You can give up that extra beer or cigarette, or postpone some equipment purchase, or cut your expected wages, but you should not give up on the advertising, it is what brings in both new and past customers, it provides you with your 'bread and butter'.

Advertising Always Do's:

Always do a grammar and a spell check on the text of an advertisement. Too many times there are little mistakes that detract from the advertisement message and make you or your company appear incredibly ridiculous.

Have at least one other person check the text and content for errors. Two or more people are better. Don't be afraid to ask an elder to review what you are doing, I will give you a prime example. In my beginning days I sent out a mailer via USPS (United States Postal Service) and I had envelopes printed with a thin black band on all edges thinking that this would attract attention, it did. My mother and father immediately informed me, after I had mailed hundreds of these that during WWII parents received notices of their loved one's demise in black edged envelopes. Needless to say, I destroyed several hundred unused envelopes.

Suppliers - Get Referrals From

If you are in the business of contracting, then you probably have a materials supplier or two and they probably have inquiries as to which they recommend as being the best person to install the products that they sell. Now, most cannot, or will not recommend a specific contractor as in doing so they are recommending one of their clients, you, against another of their clients and that is not good business, but they can allow you to place your business card on their counter along with others, and they can answer direct questions, if asked by someone that is in need of a contractor.

Basic Advertising Essentials:

Demographics. Who Looks at Your Ads?

Who are your customers? What age group, what racial group, what financial group, etc.; this information can help you determine the services and products needed by those in your geographical area. For example, you may be in a neighborhood of all middle-class Irish that are in the 20 to 40 year old group. This translates to young families, partiers, and workers that may have a need for a deck, patio, playroom, nursery, etc. and thus you can and should advertise to the needs of this group.

When Needed - Not Until:

When are your services needed? If you are in the repair end of Construction and Contracting, such as being a Roofer during a major rainstorm, then the need for your services is immediate. On dry weather days the client's roof may need repair, but he or she not only doesn't know it, or even cares, therefore you will infrequently get a call to come fix the roof. But, during that rain where the water is pouring down and destroying the bedroom furniture, you can be sure that he or she will be seeking your services.

The idea here is that most will not require help from you until the 'disaster' strikes, and then you need to have your contact information immediately available and easy to find and use, else you will lose the job.

Now, as to non-emergency construction, this is usually seasonal. People want a new patio or deck at the first sign of spring, they want a new kitchen just before the holidays, they want new carpeting and painting after the summer school vacation, etc. You have to figure out the timing of their needs, and then get your advertising out there to those that may need your products or services.

There are other categories and needs, such as when one becomes a senior and is having trouble walking, climbing, reaching, seeing, hearing, etc. this opens the doors to all sorts of home improvements for the safety of the person or persons living there, and it is a plus to you, if you can supply or fulfill the needs.

Then there is the injured or illness from sickness or from war or accident, that requires better and wider doorways, entry ramps, lighting, communications, etc. If you are in the market supplying these items, your advertising should be linked to information services that inform you of the needs of these people.

What Must Be In An Ad?

The answer is simple, something that catches a person's eye and makes him or her want to investigate further. This can be a catchword, picture, or coupon, etc. that will stand out among dozens of other ads that may also be competing for attention. *Words like* FREE, SALE, and COUPON are eye catchers that usually STOP a person in their tracks. Pictures of babies, puppy dogs, and explosions generally capture an audience's attention.

Once you find that 'key' to the public interest, use it over and over until it is no longer effective.

What Can I Leave Out?

Bad mouthing your competition and unnecessary items that do nothing to attract attention and sell your product or service. *Examples:* We are better than XYZ, they don't give you a warranty. Or, we are the world's number one contractor, a statement that you cannot prove.

Where Do I Advertise?

This is one of the more difficult questions to answer as it depends on the cost, media exposure, and what you are advertising. If you have a very *limited budget*, you will probably lean toward *flyers* or the *Internet*, and you will probably be very disappointed in the results. If your budget is large, you may lean toward billboards, radio or television spots, and again you may be disappointed. So, the answer to the question is to look to see where others in your profession are advertising, and use that, it seems to work for them, so it should work for you.

One interesting place to advertise is on the building in which your business occupies, the *signs on your building* should be situated so that traffic coming from both directions can see the signs; most place the signs on the front street side where oncoming traffic cannot see the signs until directly in front of the building. Also, is there a *traffic camera* nearby that displays your building, if so be sure your sign shows in the view, you get free advertising 24/7 this way. In the front of your building, if you have a window area, then display your services; this can be done with signs or with *CCTV, Closed Circuit Television* that has 20-second advertising spots that run 24/7. This CCTV system can be changed to reflect your latest 'sale' and it captures the attention of people whether you are open for business, or taking off for the day.

Now, once you have a build-up of clients, and you should be keeping a listing or *database* of all your clients, their addresses, phone numbers, and email addresses, then you can send them *'follow-up'* letters, which unfortunately are getting expensive, or emails which are about the least costly way to go. If sending emails, you need to get permission from your *Internet service provider* for *'bulk'* mailing, and you need to have an 'opt-out' method for the receiving clients.

Last Thing To Cut From Your Budget:
The dollars are getting tight, you cannot pay your rent or insurances, etc. and you have to cut expenses, where do you cut. Unfortunately, many cut the advertising budget first, and the beer money last, which is exactly opposite to what is needed.

When times are tough, the first thing you need to do is 'advertise' your services to bring in more paying clients that will increase your earnings. You should actually increase your advertising budget during bad times, as others may mistakenly decrease theirs and therefore, your ads will have less competition and each will stand out more, thus attracting their clients to you.

Budget % For Advertising

8

In good times when you have more work than you can handle, your advertising budget can be negligible, but I recommend at least $4.00 for each $100 of income, or 4%. In bad times, you should increase the budget to a minimum of $8.00 per $100 of income, or 8% or more. Just be sure to 'track' the results to make sure you are advertising the 'right' product or services at the time each is needed. It makes little sense to advertise new decks in December during a blizzard or when it is about to snow for two weeks.

News Media Advertising:

Bygone Era - Newspaper Classifieds?

It is fast becoming a non-media for advertising as newspaper after newspaper goes bankrupt or closes due to non-readership, and as the current generation of *seniors* dies off the readership will become near non-existent. This means that the once very popular place to advertise local contracting businesses has, or is becoming obsolete. The *Internet* has taken over, but to a local contractor, the Internet is too big, too general, too widespread for most.

Type in 'Roofer' into a *search engine* and see what you get, 2,000,000 or more names. The user has to be very specific and not only type in the word 'Roofer' but also the name of the city or town, the section, and the specific type of roof just to get the list down to 200. Then since most search engines only display 10 to 20 names per page, the user generally does not search past the first one or two pages, so if your *Internet advertisement* is on the third to tenth page, the chances are you will not be selected. The answer is to use the Internet to expand your advertising, and then advertise your Internet website in the few remaining newspapers, and on other media.

Cost of Radio and Television Ads?

The cost of an ad is fully dependent on the response and earnings gained from the advertisement. If the *advertisement cost* $10,000 and you receive 1,000 calls but only one job, then the cost of the advertisement per job gained is $10,000, but if you managed to close on all 1,000 jobs, then the cost of the ad per job gained is $10.00 per job, which is reasonable, but in this instance not probable. Thus, the answer to the cost of radio and television ads is that there is no true answer; if the ad works for you and you are satisfied with the results, then the cost was reasonable, if you were not satisfied, then the cost was excessive.

Do I recommend radio and television as an advertising medium, not really for the following reasons:

First, is that there are hundreds of radio and television stations and you must find the one that can present your message to the people you are seeking or that are most likely to purchase your product or services. More difficult than you think, due to factors like when people listen, what they are doing at the time, do they need your services, and do they have the availability to jot down your name, and contact information.

Second, is that you cannot place a single advertisement, you must place *multiple advertisements* over several days to weeks or more; it takes a 'shotgun' approach to get your message out to hundreds of people that may be looking at the very time your advertisement is broadcasting.

Third, radio and television advertising is geared toward '*product and brand recognition*', and not toward selling a specific product. If you look at most of the television advertisements you will see that it is the *Company Name* that is being hammered into your brain, not the individual product, although a product may be shown, it is only representative of what you can purchase. *Example:* A car manufacturer may show a beautiful full-loaded vehicle, but it does not directly sell that vehicle to you; the advertisement is only to show the brand and get you to enter a dealer's showroom, where you almost never see that exact vehicle that was so handsomely displayed on television.

Four, the idea behind effective advertising is to have your name there when someone wants your service. Do you really think that a potential client that needs your service is going to turn on the radio or television and watch for hours in the hope that he or she once again sees your 10 second commercial and then calls you, or do you think that the person will look to the Internet, local Yellow Pages, or local newspaper media? My bet is on the latter.

Repeat, Repeat, Repeat:

The fact that you need to have your name in front of potential buyers at the time he or she is ready to buy, means that you must advertise once and measure the effectiveness, and if the advertisement was effective, brought in jobs sufficient to make the advertising cost reasonable, then you must Repeat, Repeat, Repeat the advertisement. If you let the advertisement drift away into time, then you will see a point when the jobs that were previously generated will also 'drift' away.

Other Print Advertising Media:

Flyers:

The majority of new small business contracting firms start advertising by putting out hundreds of 8.5" x 11.0" colored paper flyers in parking lots and on telephone poles and other easy to stick it to places. This can land you in court in some instances, as many localities have made it illegal to *drive nails or staples in to telephone poles*, others communities dislike the fact that a large percentage of the flyers end up on the streets and into the sewers or runoff water drain systems.

Utility companies also have strict rules as the nails and staples while climbing the poles doing maintenance work can injure their workers. If a worker is injured, then you may find yourself footing some medical bills for that worker.

USPS Mail Advertising:

The United States Postal Service delivers millions of advertising each day across the nation, and for some companies like a supermarket or hardware store this works as it keeps the company name in front of potential clients, and it offers 'specials' that bring in customers.

For an individual or contractor, the USPS is not the best means for advertising as it cost upwards of $0.60 per each letter or flyer sent. (Cost of stamps, envelopes, paper, printing, ink, etc.) Some contractors try to beat the postage cost by directly putting letters or flyers into mailboxes, do NOT do this, it is against the law and can result in very large fines.

If you are going to use the USPS, then use Postcards for your sales pitch. Postcards can be seen by the potential clients and cost less. Each may still end up in the circular trash bin, but usually after the client sees your sales pitch.

Again, you have to send out these letters or postcards on a regular, weekly or monthly basis, or else each becomes a total waste of your hard-earned advertising dollars.

Yellow Pages:

Although the Yellow Pages are still being printed and distributed, many people today go first to their cell phone or desktop computer and a 'search engine'. You can place your ad in the Yellow Pages, and it may produce some leads, but how would you know?

Here is a trick to any advertising. Use an 'identifier' that is unique to the ad that you placed. This way you can tie the sale or lead to the ad and thus of a period calculate the effectiveness of the ad, and the cost of each customer gained from the ad.

Examples: Two identical ads, one placed in the Yellow Pages and the second in the local newspaper. Ad # 1 has 'YP-256' as the identifier and ad # 2 has 'LN-356' as its identifier. YP-256 cost $100 and brought in 5 paying clients, therefore it cost $20 for each. LN-356 cost $100 and brought in 50 paying clients, and therefore each cost $2.

Bumper Stickers:

Bumper stickers are more for bragging about your kid in school or telling a joke or two. Not really conducive to advertising your business.

Vehicle Signs:

Vehicle signs are effective if the sign is well created and easy to read from both stopped and moving vehicles. Distinctive colors of the vehicle and the signs also help as when seen it 'registers' in the mind of the viewer that 'so and so company' drives 'purple and green' vehicles. Example, almost everyone knows a USPS or U-Haul truck just from the color combination used.

Internet Advertising:

Cost of a Website?

How much does it cost to open and maintain a working *Internet* website? You can obtain an Internet website provider for as little $4.95 a month, up to hundreds per month, all depending on what the provider is providing to you. If you understand and can write some **.HTML code*, the language of the Internet, then you can purchase any of several off-the-shelf website development packages available at most stores that sell computers and computer software. The *WYSIWYG format* is easy to learn, easy to use, and provides good basic results for a cost of under $100. The *'What You See Is What You Get'* format allows you to develop web pages in simple English, and then with a push of a button convert the text and photos to *.HTML, or *Hypertext Markup Language* that can be published via your account at the Internet website provider's location.

Now, if you use a *prepackaged website service*, you will be provided with a hundred or so 'templates' that ask questions and then fills in the website pages with your answers. This is a very simple method of developing a website, but will cost you from about $40 to $100 per month, for as long as you own the Domain and use the provider. A *Domain* is your website's name on the Internet and is a must, which has to be purchased for about $10 per year. Without the Domain Name, you cannot open a website, we will cover this later in this manual.

If you decide to 'hire' a *website developer* and have him, her, or they create your site, then you are talking about spending hundreds to thousands of dollars. Those that do this are usually well funded, in business for many years, and are seeking a very complicated and professional looking site, which may be of benefit or may actually turn off customer's that are seeking 'bargain' prices.

Cost of Maintaining a Website?

The cost of maintaining a website can be as low, under $200 per year for the *Domain Name* renewal and the *Internet service provider*, and up into the tens of thousands if you have to hire professional programming services. Most will find the costs to be about $500 per year, and you should include the costs in your budgets.

Initial Programming Costs?

The initial cost is your time, if you are the *programmer*; the salary of another if you have an employee do it for you; the cost of a contracting firm is you have another company do it for you. Thus, the cost of programming is zero to tens of thousands of dollars, all depending on which route you take.

Getting Seen?

Your chances of getting seen on the *Internet* is very, very poor as there are tens of millions of Internet websites that cover the aspirations of billions of people world wide. This is why the Internet is termed, *WWW*, the *World Wide Web*. Thus, if you are advertising as a house painter on the Internet, you will be one of about 40,000,000 other house painters advertising on the Internet. So why have a website you ask, the answer is simple, you have to have a presence that your past, current, and future clients can seek out and view. In the past, the phone company *Yellow Pages* were the place to have that ever present advertisement, in the digital age, the WWW is the place.

Keywords?

Some *Internet Search Engines* look into the *HTML code* of your website pages and seek out the 'keywords', these keywords are then data based and used by the users of the search engines to find your website. For instance, a keyword can be 'Electrician' and if someone types Electrician into his or her Internet Search Engine he or she will get a list of Electricians that also used this keyword. Your job is to come up with *Unique Keywords* that your potential clients will understand and normally think of when searching for your website.

For example: AZX Electricians; this is a unique keyword and the probability is that only you will have this, but will the average person looking for an electrician know this keyword, probably not. A keyword like 'Electrical Work' may be more suited, and used by more potential clients. You can place many keywords on your website, and each web page can have a different grouping of keywords.

14

Here is a code example.

```
<meta name="keywords"
 content="newburg,electrician,wiring,lighting,soc
 kets,appliances,circuit breakers,power
 meters,gfi,service entry">
```

Note that there are no spaces between each comma and keyword, that lower case is used, and that there is usually a limit to the number of keywords that you can have on each page (keep below 25 for acceptance on most Internet search engines)

Also note that when a person types in *'Newburgh appliances'* he or she will get a listing of appliances and appliance stores in the town of Newburgh. Thus, you can with the right choice of keywords customize the potential clients search results to your company.

Description of Your Internet Page:

At the top of each Internet page you will see a description of the page, this is sometimes used by the *Internet Search Engines* for finding your website.

Example of the Code
```
<meta name="description" content="Free Electrical
 Safety Check, no obligation, contact AZX
 Electricians">
```


Page Loading Times:

Keep the code simple and limited so that your website pages load fast and accurately. Pages that take more than a few seconds to load on a clients screen will turn off the client and he or she may go to another contractor's website.

Links and Jumps:

Keep it simple, do not hide links and jumps to other pages. I have seen programmers that love to garbage up the screens with all sorts of junk that has little to do with the product, and then add links that are hidden in pictures, buried in text, and difficult to find.

15

Logos and Brand Recognitions:

The page Header or Footer should contain your logo so that it will show on every page of your business website.

Headers and Footers:

A header is a piece of computer code that is displayed on the top of each page in the website. The footer is the code that is displayed on the bottom of the page and usually contains the copyright, the Webmaster's name, the links to the FAQ, Contact, and other pages.

Page to Page Same Information:

I have seen websites that have conflicting information from page to page, different lettering type, and other items that make for confusing text and information. If you call 'xyz' a 'whatsit' on page one, do the same on all the other pages, do not change the name to a 'whoisit'.

Menus:

Most websites have a menu that allows the user to find the website page that contains the information they desire to see. Example: Location of your business, who to contact, what products do you sell, what services do you provide, etc. Menus are usually at the top right on the screen, and sometimes duplicated at the bottom.

Pictures:

Pictures tell a story about you and your products or services. Use good quality pictures that display the items, not the gal in the skimpy bathing suit behind the product.

Test the website pages on several different platforms. (A platform can be a desktop computer, a cell phone, and computer pad, and the various resolutions that each can produce) Also, there are several different web browsers on the market and each may display differently. It is no fun for the user to open a website and find that 40% of the screen is off to the right and cannot be viewed. Always design for the OLDEST Computers, not the newest.

Text Boxes and Frames:

Text boxes and frames are methods of separating specific information on a website screen. Use the same precautions as with pictures.

Pages Needed:

Most professional websites for a business should contain the following.

Copyright notice

Contact names and means of contact

Disclaimer

Content or Homepage

Sales pages - what can I do for you

Order page

Forms:

Many websites require the gathering of information from the potential client, and therefore will need a forms page. These forms can be questionnaires that help you qualify the potential client.

Order Page:

If you are selling a product on-line then you will need an Order Page that collects the client's name, address, payment information, and items being ordered. This should be followed with an 'Acceptance' page that confirms the order and allows the client to print or save a copy of the order. The codes for much of this can be obtained from the credit card company you are using gather info and payments from your clients.

Where to Advertise:

On Your Clothing:

Most contractors start out very small, and then grow as more people know of him or her, and therefore he or she usually wears *'street'* *clothing* or some other item like *painter's whites*, etc. The last thing one thinks of when starting a business is designing or purchasing a uniform, which actually should be one of the first items.

A distinctive uniform with a big *logo* on the backside will display your name and business to everyone that you pass, or who passes you while you shop, work, or travel to a client's site for the job. There are *Uniform Providers* throughout the USA, and you should be able to find one that will custom tailor a set or two for you at a reasonable price.

Figure it this way, each *newspaper ad* you buy will cost about $15 to $25 dollars and last for one to two days, a uniform costing $100 will last for one to two years or more, which therefore becomes very cost effective advertising.

On Highways:

Old fashion Billboards required that you hire a printer to print giant signs, then hire a billboard for the signs, then hire someone to glue the sign to the billboard, then pay a monthly rent on the billboard, and finally pay someone to remove the sign or change it when required. Most contractors cannot afford this sequence of events as it can run into the hundreds or thousands.

Newer Billboards are electric and computer controlled. All you need is to submit to the owners a small high-quality graphic that can be converted electronically into a television type screen picture. Your advertisement can then be displayed over and over without any install or removal cost. It can be scheduled to the dates and times that your potential clients may see it, and it can be made to 'move' just like a television picture. The thing to remember is that like the sign on your building, traffic is moving and people may not be able to copy all the information; thus, keep it simple, direct, understandable, and memorable; i.e. "Jakes Professional Pool Care".

On-job sticker

Add to the furnace, water heater, etc. Always add a sticker or some other identifier to your job so that if the client needs your help or wants you to do more, he or she can easily find your information. I have had cases were I was hauled into court by clients of a competitor, all because his or her client did not have access to his or her name, and 'thought' I was the contractor that messed up their job.

Construction Referral Services:

Back in my contracting days I had a website named 'PhiliContractorsMall.com © (2011) and I offered local contractors FREE advertisement on my website. All they had to do was to be willing to post their credentials and contracting history so that my website clients could feel comfortable in hiring them. One year of advertising the plan, handing out thousands of flyers at the local hardware and building supply, and not one taker. Several years later we now have Angie's List™ and several other contractor referral sites that you can join, if you wish.

Here is another idea; many towns have a NextDoor™ app or website that you can use to pinpoint your advertising services directly to the neighborhood that you service.

Vehicle Advertising:

Vehicle Paint Jobs:

Painting your vehicle so that it stands out in a crowd can help get you name recognition. But, be careful to not go overboard with super complex paint designs that hide the message, your ad.

Also, is a $ 3,000 specialty paint job worth the cost, will it bring in more clients, and how would you know if it did? Perhaps a $150 stick on printed sign with your name, what you do, and a contact number would be better. Don't forget to add your contractor's license number if you have one.

Age of the Vehicle:

Nothing wrong with driving an old vehicle, car or truck, if it is kept looking clean and decent. Drive up to a client's house with the vehicle covered in mud, dented fenders, broken tail light and you can forget being considered for any job at that client's place. Maybe renting a car, van, or truck for the day would present a better picture of success.

Referrals - Word of Mouth:

One of the items taught in any sales class is that 'word of mouth' is the best advertising as it costs little to nothing money wise, and can produce excellent results. But.....

Upside:

The upside of 'word of mouth' advertising is the lack of cost money wise and that if, if you are doing a good job people will *recommend* you to others that may hire you to do similar jobs for them. This means that you may obtain a client without paying for advertising, thus saving money, and thus increasing profits on the job. But....

Downside:

There may be a downside to 'word of mouth' and it is one that can destroy you and your business within a very short period. The fact is that if you do a good job for someone, he or she may tell others, but if you do a bad job, he or she will almost always tell others. You do not need to be *'bad mouthed'* by a client that feels that you did him or her wrong in any way; it is bad for business.

Relatives:

You can hope that your relatives tell their friends and coworkers about you and your company, but do not depend on it happening, and do not be disappointed if it does not happen. *Relatives* are frequently the last people that will recommend you, they may not know how good you are at your job, or even what your job is, and therefore will hesitate to put themselves in a position of 'goofing' up by recommending you and then having to explain to their friends about your 'poor' performance or lack of knowledge in the thing they thought you knew.

Neighbors:

Ditto, this is about the same as having your relative recommend you, except now if you do 'goof' up it will be around the entire neighborhood within hours.

Friends:

The question here is who is your friend? Some 'friends' are people that are envious of you and your success, and therefore will covertly do what he or she can to discredit you with others. Other friends are actually friends and want to see you succeed and will help spread the word that you are in business. You have to do one very important thing with relatives, neighbors, and friends, and that is to let each know what you do.

The "*I do plumbing*" is not enough as there are rough-in plumbing jobs, finished plumbing jobs, industrial plumbing, commercial plumbing, water, gas, fuel line plumbing etc. You have to be specific as "I do new or replacement plumbing in residential kitchens in the xyz area of the town."; now they will feel more comfortable in recommending you and you will not have to explain to them why you turned down a $1,000,000.00 gas line plumbing job in Egypt.

Pro-Bono Work:

This is a form of 'word of mouth' advertising that will take some of your time and energy, and maybe some dollar cost for travel and materials, but it can help get your name out there. Doing some 'free' or 'pro-bono' work for an organization that is helping people can give you experience and help you gain respect from those that can see your work first hand and thus, feel comfortable in recommending you to those that will pay you for your talents. Many towns, cities, counties, and such have *low-income aid organizations*, and many welcome volunteer help.

Also try relief organizations that are helping people after a storm or flood or fire, and try *Habitat for Humanity*. Be sure to ask for and receive a letter of recommendation for your good work when the job is completed.

Joining Organizations:

This form of 'word of mouth' is one of the easiest to obtain, providing you are a legitimate contractor doing good work. It may cost you for 'dues' or some other item like a newsletter, but being able to say you are a member of a *professional organization*, and displaying their logo on your uniform, truck, ads, website, and such is powerful to those seeking an honest professional contractor.

Local Organizations:

If you have the credentials, then by all means join the local *VFW*, *American Legion, Masons*, etc. as doing so will get you known to the community and people in communal organizations tend to recommend each other and back each other in the event of problems or needs. Again, make sure they know precisely what you do for a living and what you can do for them and their friends, coworkers, and relatives.

Celebrity Endorsements:

Not everyone can get an *endorsement* from a big *television* or movie star, but if you can it can rocket your business to new heights of success. People that have been mentioned on television have at times seen a thousand fold increase in business, within seconds to days of having their business or product or service featured by a television celebrity. Use caution though, as like any other word of mouth advertising, if your product or service fails or is poorly recommended, it can be the end of your business, within seconds to days. Also, always get *written permission* to use the celebrity's name or show in any future advertisements, less they may come visit you with an attorney.

Seminars and Demonstrations:

Whether paid or not, you can promote your product or services to many by providing demonstrations and seminars. *Example*: You are good at woodworking and thus give a Sunday afternoon demonstration at the local home improvement store in your town.

Clinics:

Offering free clinics for your services can bring you from zero to dozens of potential clients, but remember these people are looking for 'free' information and thus, are not overly willing to spend their hard-earned cash on you. You have to provide enough information to make it worth their time to come and listen to you, and also provide some information on what you can do for them, in the event they cannot do it themselves or if they get into trouble, or find a job to taxing.

For example: As a Roofer you can show people how to properly install new asphalt shingles, and many will go home and do it properly, but there will be those that cannot take the weight of the shingles while climbing a ladder, or the heat of working on the roof, or that may feel the job is too dangerous once started. It is at these times that you want them to call you, and your clinic has already told them that you are the expert, and you gave out information on what you do and the approximate cost, and you made sure that he or she has your flyer and business card.

Clubs:

As with clinics and demonstrations, many clubs, including *senior clubs*, routinely bring in outside speakers that can talk for 15 to 45 minutes on a specific subject of interest to the group. I gave 45-minute talks to Senior Groups on how to spot 'con' jobs and prevent being cheated by crooks and others that would take advantage. I limited the talks to 45 minutes as from experience I found that interest wanes after this period, and therefore becomes ineffective. *Flyers* and *business cards* are handed out at the beginning of the talks, along with a summary of my business and what is being discussed; this way each listener takes notes and thus tends to keep the paperwork much longer than if given out afterwards.

Business Cards:

Always have a business card available, it may end up in the trash, but many do keep the cards for future use. A good business card has your company name, telephone and *Internet contact information*, and hours of operation. A personal name or short description of the business also works, as does color and style of the card that displays professionalism. *Examples*: Member of the *BBB* or *Licensed and Bonded*, etc.

During and After the Job:

You are wiring up an addition to the client's home and you notice that the bathroom and kitchen does not have *GFI* (*Ground Fault Interrupters*) as required by code, thus you have an *opportunity to sell more* of your services to this homeowner. When do you do this, after you get back to your office, or now? The answer is NOW. You have the client and you have the client's attention, and he or she is seeing how you work and that you are a professional that knows what you are doing, therefore you are one-up on your competition, so why wait and give the client time to call your competition and risk losing the additional work?

Your job is not only to do the work, but is to sell, sell, sell all the time, and this means looking for the advantage all the time. You and your employees must do this, and should be educated on the services you can offer, as opportunity is all around, if you can see it.

During a Callback:

No one likes a Callback, as it cuts into profits and can easily turn a profitable job into a total loss, and therefore you should be very careful the first time, and double check that your work was properly done the first time. But as all construction contractors know or have experienced, callbacks will happen; some purchased and installed product will fail, or you or a worker forgot to do something, or your contract was not 'iron-clad' and the client found a loophole that allows him or her to get more or pay less, etc.

There are two ways to handle a callback, with pleasure or with anger, and if done with anger it will be noticed by the client and may cost you future jobs and more callbacks from this client. If you handle the job with pleasure, on time, and with a professional attitude the client will generally understand that things happen, make allowances, and if you handled it right, recommend you as being an honest and reliable contractor.

Now, here comes the place for an *additional sale*, as you are leaving ask the client if your response was to his or her satisfaction, and if no, why and make it right; if yes then thank the client and let him or her know that you are available for their needs…..like… and here is where you point out that you can do other work for him or her, work that you have noticed that needs to be done. *For an example*, if you put in a kitchen floor, then there may be a possible job of replacing the dining room flooring to match; after all the new kitchen floor made the dining room floor look worn and old. Remember, sell, sell, and sell.

Construction Ads and Internet Sites

What to Look For:

Some will think that the following chapter is "silly"; for who would run an advertisement and forget to include *vital information*. Well it has happened, one company, not in construction, actually ran an advertisement that only had the name of the company's product, their marketing 'thought' that everyone knew about it and them; they were dead wrong to the tune of millions in wasted advertising dollars. After all, if 'everyone' knew about it and them, then 'why' advertise? Thus, this chapter provides not only the 'what to look for' items of an ad, but can be used as a *checklist* for making sure that all necessary information is included in the advertising on which you are spending hard-earned dollars and counting on to bring in more.

In alphabetical order:

Ad on Vehicle Matches Ad on Internet:

Does your *Internet pages advertisement* match the advertisements that you are displaying on your vehicle and in other media? A person looking for you may see your *printed advertisement* around town and decide to look you up on the Internet, which is a good place to present your 'complete' services. The sign on the truck may say that you are a Carpenter, but the Internet can clarify this information by pointing out that you do Rough Carpentry, Finished Carpentry, Trim work, and Decorative Trim Carpentry.

Thus, as soon as the person opens your *Homepage* (*Index or Content page*), he or she will see that he or she has come to the correct Website, the *Logo*, name, and other information matches the information he or she saw elsewhere. If you have a different listed name or a different Logo or claim in bold letters to be a Flooring Expert, the viewer may think that he or she made a mistake and thus, search elsewhere leaving your advertisement to drift in the vapors of cyberspace.

Archives:

Have you been updating your website with 'tips' on how to do things or other information that may be of use to your clients? If so, you will eventually be adding item pages and having to do something with the old pages; the suggestion is that you set up a menu link on the [Home] page that takes the user to a [*Archives Menu*] page. This allows your clients to view all the free information you are providing, without having to load each story along with the [Home] page; which makes for a cleaner and easier to use site.

Area of Operation:

Advertising is for capturing the client at the moment that he or she needs a service or item, and he or she expects to find this right next-door. Contracting work is small business for most; the owner works within a confined radius of the business home or workshop. This is usually within a ten (10) to twenty (20) mile radius, and therefore all advertising should be aimed at that area.

It makes no sense to advertise that you install water heaters in a magazine that covers the entire state or geographical region, the cost of the ad is huge and the majority of potential clients will be well outside your working range. Thus, shop for and use less expensive advertising that targets your immediate town, neighborhood, or country.

Awards:

Have you or your company received any awards for your service or contributions to the industry? If so, you should make copies of the award certificates and post these on your website to show that you are a responsible person or business.

Blog:

Many companies have found that by adding a '*Comment*' page section to their *Internet websites* that they get a following of 'experts' that like to speak out and try to help others with their problems, and such. This is one form of a Blog, the other is where you post to the Internet your ideas and suggestions for those reading. Either way you gain recognition and potential clients, but remember that you do open yourself up to *criticism* and those that are hostile to you, or those persons that feel harmed by your company and thus will post their negative opinions on your Comment pages for all to see. Also, be careful of those that misuse the pages for their possible *unlawful activities* like porn or con jobs.

Bonded:

People like to be secure in the knowledge that if something goes wrong with the job being done that they have some recourse for getting the job completed, and knowing that the contractor being hired is *licensed and bonded* goes a long way in making people feel secure. Thus, if you are bonded, then state this in your advertising.

Bragging Rights:

Do you claim bragging rights? Can you? May you? If you or your company has received a *certificate of achievement*, or a positive newspaper write-up, or some other item that says you are 'great', then this becomes a positive advertising message that can bring in additional business, but do you have permission to use these in your advertisements?

You should ask for and receive written permission to use these 'bragging' points, before you actually use each. *For example*: You have applied to one of the *professional organizations* listed in the Appendix, but have not yet received the acceptance, thus you are not permitted to say you belong to 'such and such', and it can become an embarrassment to do so and then have to remove such claims.

Cell Phone Number:

There was a time when cell phones were the pride of the rich and elite, the phones were expensive and service was confined to small areas of the country; today with communication satellites flying overhead by the hundreds and cell phones costing less than a carton of cigarettes, a *cell phone* is a must. It not only keeps you in contact with your base of operations and other employees, but also with potential clients.

Before the Cell Phone, a client would call your *Landline phone number* and if you were on a job, he or she would either hang up and try later, or leave a message and then start down the listing of your contracting specialty in the phone book. The chances are that you would lose that potential customer to another contractor; but now you can take the call, and make arrangements for a meeting, thus opening up the door to a sale. Moral put the Cell Phone Number in your advertisements and especially on the *Internet* Page.

Do so in the *Footer Page*. (Information that remains the same and is on the bottom of each page of the website).

Credit Cards One Can Use, With Pictures

Do you offer your client's credit? If not, then you are losing an opportunity for attracting clients, especially in economic distressed times. One-way to easily offer credit is to use an Internet service like *Paypal* ®. Millions of *Internet users* have a Paypal account or know of Paypal and trust their services, and therefore you can take deposits, do billing, and set up payment terms through Paypal for these people.

Paypal does accept *major credit cards* like Mastercard and Visa and can transfer funds from their, your, service accounts to and from your bank account. It is a safe, easy to use, and trusted method of payment, thus increasing your sales possibilities.

Date of Ad or Website:

If you put an ad or special promotion item on your website or in any printed advertising, then be sure to include the dates of the promotional, you don't want people coming to you with a three year old ad demanding 'xyz' at 'xyz' price that is totally out of date and that will cost you more than the job is worth.

Daytime Phone Number:

Where can you be reached during the day? Many small construction contractors and handymen are on the job during the day and thus, not at their home or office where their primary business telephone is located. Thus, you should make sure that you provide a daytime telephone number where those seeking you can find you. This can be done with an answering service, or a cell phone service.

Departments With Contact Info:

Is your business large enough to have departments? You know like a Sales Department, a Design Department, a Credit Department, a

Marketing Department, a Delivery Department, or an HR (Human Resources) Department; if so great you are really doing well and growing; but most small contracting firms do NOT have these departments, the owner does it all. So in your advertisements or on your website do you include 'contact' information for these departments? Although I do not condone this, some small business owner's do claim to have several departments in an effort to make them, and thus their business look larger than they or it actually is. They use different names for the heads of the departments, and different mailroom or contact numbers, and 'fakes' it, but it works, until someone finds out and spreads the word.

Design and 3D

Do you have CAD (Computer Aided Drafting) capabilities? If so can you do 3D drawings? If you are doing remodeling, room additions, landscaping, etc. then you have an advantage over much of your competition and you need to advertise this advantage.

Discounts for?

Why give discounts, and if doing so, on what? So many in an attempt to bring in business will offer discounts, the advertisements show 30, 40, up to 70% off on Saturday Only type ads. Well, as a client I have to ask, if you can give me a 70% discount on Saturday, then why can't you give me the discount on Monday, Tuesday, Wednesday, Thursday, and Friday?

If you are giving discounts, then do not give a discount on the service, but instead do so on the materials being used; that way you can always say you are temporarily overstocked on an item due to a storm, customer backing out of a deal, volume discount received, etc. This then suggests that the discount is a one-time thing, and that you are passing on the savings to your potential clients.

Discounts for Seniors and Veterans:

Do you give discounts to *senior citizens* or *Veterans* in an effort to capture that part of the market? If so, then have it spelled out that you do give discounts and how much. Also, specify the age that you consider a person to be a senior, some feel it is age 55, others 60, 62, or

65. Are there specific jobs or days of the week or other limitations on when a senior citizen may receive the discounts?

Educational Materials:

Many contractors find that giving away 'free' knowledge to potential clients can lead to increased jobs, after all if you are the 'teacher' then you must know what you are doing and thus, *you are the expert*. So, the idea is to present yourself or your contracting company as the experts in the field by publishing short one-page educational materials on your website. *For example:* A landscaper can do a page on how to shape the land for best water retention and plant growth. The more articles you publish on your website, the more valuable the site becomes and thus, the more recommendations you may receive.

eMail address:

When you contract for a new website you usually receive one to many possible email addresses of your creation. For example: Csr@mycontracting.com where *Csr* stands for Customer Service Representative, the @ symbol tells the Internet that this is an Email address, the *mycontracting* is your company and website name, and *.com* is the Internet classification of your Website. You can have different names for the wording before the @ sign, but not afterward. Thus, you may have Sales@mycontracting.com, Marketing@mycontracting.com, Billing@mycontracting.com, Appointments@mycontracting.com , etc. These are all valid email addresses.

You can also have a 'forwarding' box or email account that is linked to all the other addresses, thus if you set up Forwardtome@mycontracting.com and link the Sales@mycontracting.com, Marketing@mycontracting.com, Billing@mycontracting.com, and Appointments@mycontracting.com emails to it, all emails will come to the Forwardtome@mycontracting.com account.

Emergency Number:

If you have a contracting service that can be considered an 'emergency' service, then you need to publish the 'Emergency Contact Number' on your website. *For example:* You are a plumber that will come out at 4 AM in the morning to stop a major water leak that is flooding a basement or you are a window glass person that will come out during a storm on Sunday and replace the window that was just destroyed by a tree branch. Potential and prior clients will appreciate knowing that you, among all those others, will respond to their need at the time of their need.

Employment, if offered

If you are accepting resumes and employment applications, then you should have a separate web page that details the jobs, the qualifications needed, and the procedure you use for setting up interviews. You do not need to list the optional items like salaries and benefits, but if may get you more applicants if you do.

Equipment Limitations:

You may be doing a type of work that can be for a local residential area or for a commercial or industrial area. Let's say you are doing driveway paving, and you advertise that you are in the Paving Business. The question is do you have a small four-foot wide paving machine or roller that can handle an 80 square foot driveway being covered in asphalt, or do you have a 8 to 10 foot wide professional paving machine and roller that can handle a 500,000 square foot shopping center parking lot? Do you have the equipment for adding street drain culverts, or for doing line stripping? Hot asphalt or cold patch?

You advertisement should specify the *maximum size jobs* that you can efficiently and profitably accomplish; this will help prevent miscommunication between your company and potential clients, thus saving time and energy for both parties.

Evening Phone Number:

Many people work during the day and shop for contracting services at night. Thus, do you have an evening telephone or contact number and when is it answered; up to what time and on what days of the week. *For example:* Evening phone 1-222-555-1212 from 7 pm to 9 pm M-S, closed on Sundays. Just be sure that there is someone there to answer during the specified hours, to not answer will remove you from that potential client's list of service providers.

F.A.Q.

Frequently Asked Questions. This website section is optional, but will allow you to make up a page of information that can help eliminate calls that are frequently asked. *For example,* do you *warrant* your work, or do you have *insurance,* etc. You use the FAQ page to post these questions and your answer to each, thus providing a simple way of answering your potential client's questions without actually speaking to the client.

This has the advantage of freeing up some of your time as you are not answering telephone calls that are asking these questions, but it is also a possible disadvantage in that you are NOT in direct contact with potential clients, and therefore may be missing an opportunity to find out his or her needs and how you can fulfill these needs. Thus, be careful of the Q & A that you post, you want to inform without losing sales.

Fax Number:

Fax machines are going away, but many businesses still use these as full pages of information can be transmitted between machines. Attorneys and Real Estates rely on Fax machines for *contractual paperwork transfers* that can handle both typed and handwritten text and line-art to photo pictures.

Note that in 2019 there are software programs that can be used for 'secure' documentation transfers. Do an Internet search for "Secure Document Transfer" and you will find dozens of workable solutions.

If you have a Fax machine, by all means include the telephone number in your advertisements, it may result in more jobs being closed as you can send your Fax machine equipped client *written estimates, conception pictures* of how you think the finished job will appear, sample and completed *contracts, warrantees, blue* or *white* prints, and other pertinent information that can close the deal.

Financing:

One possible advertising that can make a difference is the availability of customer financing for the job to be done. Most people do save for a small project, but when it comes to the major repairs or construction like doing a new roof or building a two-car garage, they are usually lacking the cash for the job, and therefore require a loan of some sort.

If you can provide *Credit Union* or *Bank* or other financing, then you should be advertising this fact, and part of your sales pitch should be the availability and the cost of financing, including the down payment, progress payments, the final sign-off payment, and the period terms and interest rates. As said elsewhere, you can offer low cost credit via *MasterCard* or *Visa* or by going through websites like *Paypal* ®.

Follow Up:

This is good *customer relations* and good business in that you wait a few days after the job is completed and then call your client and ask if he or she is satisfied with the job that was done. He or she will usually say yes, sometimes even if he or she is not, but the yes answer gives you an opportunity to ask if you can supply any other items to him or her. Listen to the voice, and look for any signs of discontent, and if found then carefully feel out the person as to what was not done to his or her perfection.

Additionally, follow up a month or two later with a postcard, or if it is close to a *holiday* a *card* for that holiday. This shows that you care and that you appreciated his or her business, and it keeps your name on the front burner if and when something else that you can do is needed.

Free Checklist for You:

Free checklist on the Website. Many people think that a job is simple and can be done for pennies on the dollar, when you as the expert contractor know otherwise. Therefore, on your website you should include a check listing that displays to the potential client the *complexities of the job*, and thus possibly discouraging him or her from doing it themselves, and thus hiring you.

For example: If the client is adding a closet to his or her bedroom, your checklist may include questions that ask if there is enough space, (you

33

give minimum space requirements for a suit, etc.), whether electrical lighting is needed, whether the closet needs to be insulated for weather or sound, whether it will be cedar lined or carpeted, if the door will have two or three hinges, if the door will have a lock, can the trim be matched up with the room's remaining trim, what color and type of paint, will there be a mirror on the door, will the door open without obstruction, is there existing wiring or plumbing in the wall where the door is to be, etc.

This is enough to get most people thinking that the job may be too complicated for him or her and since you were 'smart' enough to ask the questions, maybe you should be dong the job.

Free Guides and Info:
Like the checklist, you can offer free guides on how to do the job, and if you do, you should be detailed for someone will try to follow your guide and if he or she fails, it will be your fault. But if he or she succeeds, he or she will tell everyone about where they too can obtain professional advice. Most will take one look, figure it is too much work, and give you a call.

GPS Coordinates:
Ground Position Satellites circle the earth 24/7 and provide to within a few feet locations of the item being sought. Thus, if you have a '*brick and mortar*' business, a business with a permanent storefront where people can visit during working hours, then the GPS coordinates should be listed on your website. More and more people rely on the GPS in their vehicles for finding the location of a business or other spot, and eventually we will all be wearing devices that pinpoint our locations to within inches.

Green or Environmental Statement:
In recent years the public has gotten acclimated to saving energy, stopping pollution, recycling, and conservation of water, materials, etc. This *Green Movement* is widespread and although politically a sore spot for some, it is here and you will do good to advertise that you and your company are or are going Green.

Thus, do you recycle the packaging in which the items you are installing are delivered, or do you use recycled building material, etc.? If so, be sure to include this in your advertising, it will put you a notch above some of your competition. Just do not lie about it, if you do not qualify as a member of the Green Movement, then saying you do will get you in hot water with your clients if you don't.

Green Remodeling:

Do you do new construction, repairs, or remodeling using recycled materials and energy conservative product and techniques? Yes, then by all means tell your clients that you are qualified to do Green Construction, and if you are certified.

Home Page:

Websites that start with black screens or movies?

To an older citizen or a poorer citizen that does NOT have *high-speed Internet*, the wait time for loading the homepages of many websites is cumbersome; to the point that I and many like me will 'turn off' and 'tune out', thus not seeing what you have to offer and avoiding spending money at your establishment.

Faster loading of the 'first or *Home*' *screens* will pull in the viewer and allow him or her to see what you are offering. Include links to directions, hours of operation, parking, etc. this tells the viewer, and potential visitor and spender that you took the time to care.

Yes, I understand that your *programmer* or programming staff likes to 'show off' with tons of movies, plentiful *graphics*, and code that could choke a horse, but you must consider your clients and their needs, not your programmers skills at making something 'pretty'; but in doing so is losing clients for you.

I worked for one company that paid over $1,300,000 to a battery of programmers to create the company website, it was pretty, the initial entry page looked like a Picasso painting and the user had to 'find' the links to the other pages like if he or she was doing a picture puzzle. The site failed as it should have, and a $30 dollar template was used instead, it worked fine and did what it was designed to do, bring in customers.

Websites, Finding Information?

Finding information is one of the more important concerns of a user that is about to spend his or her hard-earned money visiting your place of business.

The usual brochure, mailer, website *URL (Internet address)*, *Chamber of Commerce*, or other advertisement contains a highlighted description of your business, the location, and maybe the hours of operation and the cost. Most do not contain the specifics of the business, and therefore one has to go to the website for that information.

Once on the website one hopes to obtain information that will aid in the decision to visit the business, and aid in the decision to use your business. Unfortunately, many of the websites do NOT contain the proper information, or make it difficult to find the information.

What are needed are clear directions to information on where the business is physically located, to whom the business is geared, the parking facilities, the hours of operation, the best hours or days to attend, the availability of restrooms, and to handicapped ramps, parking, and facilities; the particulars of the business, and if there are any specific situations that can be of concern to the parents of children, the adult seniors, and those that do not understand or speak American English.

Links to the proper web pages should all be provided on the first or Index or Content page of the website. Tip, the website should have a single 8.5" x 11" printable text page that provides the necessary information, that way the visitor can click one button and print the page for his or her personal use

Hours of Operation:

Be sure to include your hours of operation and dates to call or on which you are receiving clients. If you are making evening sales calls, then state this. If you have an answering service, then state the hours in which the answering service is available and approximately when you will return the potential clients calls.

Example: Hours of Operation - Monday–Friday, 8:00 a.m.–5:00 p.m.

How Can We Benefit You:

Be sure to include a paragraph or even a page on how and why the potential client may benefit by using your product or service as compared to someone else's.

How Did You Hear About Us?

Have a short survey form that asks the reader and potential client how they found you. This can be a listing of items like Newspaper, Flyer, Word of Mouth, etc. with checkboxes that they can check. Ask for their email address, but do NOT make it or any other information mandatory. People want to 'shop' without the threat of you calling them 30-seconds after they look at your ad.

How Long In Business:

I love the advertisement that states 'Our company has 100 years of experience'. First question is '*Experience in what?*', the second is how many employees, 100 with each having 1 year of experience in something? If you are going to state things like experience then be specific with the type of experience and the actual number of years you or the company has. Been in business since 1950, then state this, it shows that you are probably well respected and sought after. Have 100 years experience in mason work between five of you, then state this as it is, "We have a combined 100 years of experience among our five highly skilled masons."

http 404 page not found - check all hyperlinks

This is an annoying factor when searching for information; the client clicks on a link only to get a '404 page not found' error message. Check your website frequently for situations that can be a bother to your clients, for outdated information, and for things like spelling errors.

Ideas:

Present your potential clients with 'ideas'. Example, you are selling driveway paving, so show pictures of the various pavers, concrete toppings, asphalt toppings, curves, lighting, and edging that can be installed. This can turn a simple $1,000 job into a beautiful $1,500 job that your client and his friends and family will enjoy for years.

If You Can, Updates on The Actual Job Being Done, Daily:

Keep your client informed of the progress and any problems that you occur. It is not nice to work for a week on a major project and then tell your client that 'Millions of Termites' are eating his or her home and it will cost an extra $10,000 for the repairs. Especially if you knew this on day one!

Insured:

Post the notice that you and your company are fully insured and comply to local and state requirements for doing the type of work you are doing.

Internships:

If you offer internships then by all means put a page on your website that tells prospective interns how to contact you and what qualifications are needed. Provide the dates and times of interviews and the dates that the internship spans.

Jobs:

Are you seeking *employees*? If so, then you should have a [Home] page link to a [Employment] page where you have a listing with descriptions of the jobs available and the employee qualifications wanted. You should present an address to which the potential employee can apply by sending his or her resume or application. Add to the page a statement of when you will get back to he or she with an appointment or rejection.

Landline Phone:

If you have a landline phone be sure to list it and to monitor the calls that may have been sent to Voicemail. Empty your Voicemail box frequently.

Liability Insurance:

Clients will be relieved to read that you have liability insurance, and many clients will not hire contractors that do not have insurance.

License Number:

Clients will be relieved to read that you have a business license, and many clients will not hire contractors that do not have a business license, but also be aware that you may need a Contractors' License and it too should be displayed. Check with your local and state authorities for the proper licenses and how each must be displayed.

Logo:

Your logo should display on every page of your website. It can be part of the Header or Footer, but it should be displayed and immediately recognized as being YOUR Logo.

Logo Statement "We Are The Best"

A logo statement like 'We are the Best' should not be used as it can be easily proven that you are NOT the best. Use a statement like 'Quality you can Trust'.

Maintenance Schedule:

If you are selling a product that needs periodic servicing like a Water Heater or Air Conditioner, then put a suggested maintenance schedule on your website. This will attract people that are nervous about their home's equipment and thus seek advice, and eventually help.

Map to Brick and Mortar Building:

A vast majority of construction contractors work from home or out of a truck and do NOT have a commercial building, but if you do, and it is open to walk-in traffic, then by all means put a map to your site on your website. Include the days and hours open, the parking situation, the physical address, and the GPS address.

Memberships:

If you are a member in good standing in a professional organization, then state this somewhere on your website.

Minimum or Maximum Size Jobs:

Save yourself and your potential clients time, state the size of the jobs that you will accept. No sense advertising that you do commercial painting if you can't paint the exterior of a ten-story building.

Name of Contact Person:

If you have more than one person working for you, then list the person, his or her job title, and job function along with the proper contact information. Example: Nancy in Billing at 555-1212.

Newsletters:

If you offer a newsletter, then make a page that can be used by your clients for signing up for the newsletters. Provide a sample newsletter so the client can get a feel for what he or she will be receiving each week, month, etc. Or, set-up an Archive area on the website and archive all your past newsletters by date and main subject or theme.

Our Process:

List out step by step what a potential client has to do to secure an estimate, and what is required if the job is accepted. Example: To add on an addition there must be architectural drawings, permits, building inspections, an occupancy certificate, and certain fees paid. The exact fees, timing, and such may not be known, but the fact that these items are required will be helpful to the potential client and may prevent misunderstandings during the building process.

Partners:

If you are a partnership or corporation, then you should put all the members on your website.

PDF File Size and Download Estimated Times, Before Clicking

If you are offering a document that can be downloaded, then put the file size and estimated download time on the site next to the [Download] button. Newer computers are fast, but many people are still using older units and to download a 100 Megabit file can be time consuming and annoying.

Press Releases:

Have you gotten a good write-up from a local newspaper or media station? If so, ask permission and if granted post it on your website.

Privacy:

If you are accepting potential client's names, addresses, account numbers, phone numbers, email addresses, etc. then you MUST put a privacy statement on your website and do everything you can to prevent this information from getting into the wrong hands. Keep your virus software up to date, and if possible store client information off-line.

Products Used, With Logos if Possible:

Using brand 'xyz' paints, then put a picture of it on your website and be sure to specify that it is 'xyz' paint.

Referred By:

One way to gain extra customers is to ask existing customers to refer you and your company to others. You can do this and offer a 5% or whatever discount to the person making the referral, if the referral results in a sale. You can have a 'Referral' page on your site for this.

Residential Services:

Specify if you only do residential work, commercial work, or both.

Safety Awards Or ?

Have you received an award or commendation? If so, put it on your website if you feel it will attract clients or ease your client's mind about hiring you.

See Our Advertisements At...:

Are you advertising in more than one media, if so let people know.

Selling Ads For Others:

This is one of those should I or not decisions that you need to make. There are websites that you can access that provide tens of *thousands of advertisements* that you can place on your website pages and in which you may earn money. These '*click to earn a commission*' type sites give you a penny or some other amount for each time a person clicks on the published advertisement and accesses that advertiser's website.

These companies, which include some major book sellers, use a code that you have to enter into your web page, and if your client accesses the page the code goes out to their site, grabs their logo or advertising and returns it to your page for display. The time it takes for this to happen can be very short, almost instantaneous, or very long, and this can be a bother to your customers that only want to see what you offer.

Also, from experience it has been found that when you are earning some reasonable commissions, the code changes without your knowledge and although your customers are still clicking on these advertisements, you are no longer earning any commissions.

Then you have the problem of your clients clicking on these advertisements, and thus leaving your website never to return. Not good for your sales.

You use your judgment, but my recommendation is that if you are not fully in control of what is advertised on your website, you are setting yourself up for a loss.

Services Offered:

You may have a beautiful advertisement and website, but have you told your story? To say you do Finished Carpentry may be understood by you and some potential clients, but to others, Finished Carpentry can be considered as what? You should educate your potential clients as to what exactly you do, window trim, door trim, baseboards, cabinet trim, etc. this helps your potential clients to determine if you are the proper person for their needs, and it puts you ahead of the listing of potential competitors.

Tip, do not falsely claim that you can do 'such and such' in an effort to gain customers, as it will be easily apparent once the job is started that you lied, and this will cost you in the long haul. *Word of Mouth* will let all know not to believe you or your advertising.

Sitemap:
This is a mapping or listing of all the pages on your website and is not usually necessary. Some programmers feel that it helps them and you and the clients determine the number and type of pages on the website. It can be automatically generated at the push of a button using many website code generators.

Terms Of Use:
This is a standard form that you can copy off the Internet by accessing most websites, not really legal as it is copyrighted, but many do it and no one seems to complain. The *Terms of Use* is for those accessing and using your website for their informational purposes, or to contact you, which is the preferred use.

Here is where some get into trouble, the website provides a *'Comment'* or *'Blog'* page where the clients can enter their comments or questions. There are people that will use your comment or blog area for their purposes, usually for peddling *sex or sexual products* or activities. Thus, you MUST not only have a Terms of Use that legally can be used against this predators, but you MUST also check the pages daily to find and remove the objectionable materials, do not do so will be very bad advertising for your site.

Testimonials:

43

If one of your prior customers writes you a *Thank you* or other 'nice job' type note, then ask that person if you can use, publish, the note on your website and give their name as the person doing the testimonial. This is a form of *Word of Mouth* advertising and can go far in helping you obtain more clients.

Thank You For Visiting The Website:

Always provide a small thank you for visiting the website paragraph on the first page, preferably on the *Footer*, and also be sure to send an acknowledgement thank you for those that filled out your *Contact Page* or sent you an *email*. Once the thank you page has been made, most *Internet Providers* have a means for it to automatically be sent as each person accesses your email or other Contact information.

Time Open or Taking Calls:

You may have *24/7/365 access* for your potential and existing clients, but the chances are you do not. You need your free time to enjoy life, take holidays, take vacations, go shopping for materials, etc. Therefore, you should provide your clients with a set schedule of when you are open for business and for when you are taking calls. Most people will understand, as they too want their free time. The key is to not make it so difficult that people cannot or will not spend the time and energy trying to contact you. Many contracting services hire the services of an *answering service* that can take calls, determine the needs, and direct the potential clients properly. Your many have an *answering machine*, but if you do not specify when you check it daily, many potential clients will defer and call your competition.

Time to Contact You:

Working all day and do not want to answer phone calls, then specify on your website the hours in which you accept calls. Make it a range like from 7 PM to 10 PM Monday thru Friday.

Toll Free Phone Number:

If you are regional in your endeavors, then you may be out of the *local or zoned calling* zone for many of your clients, therefore you may offer a toll free 800 numbers. This does two things for you, first being you may get more calls for your services, and second, it makes you look like a larger company that can be trusted. Check with your telephone carrier for rates and restrictions.

Twitter And Facebook Addresses:

If you are *dealing with the younger generations*, then you may need a presence on the major social networks like *Twitter* and *Facebook*, but be careful; you can be charged for *commercial advertising* on some social networking websites. Twitter and Facebook are copyrighted and registered names, and thus you are at their mercy if you use each.

Type of Contracting, Professional Commercial or Residential:

Be sure to specify the type of contracting you do, be it residential, commercial, or industrial. The specification tends to display your qualifications, adherence to the codes, and professionalism in the way you operate. Most industrial concerns will not hire a residential contractor, while most homeowners will not seek out a commercial or industrial contractor.

Union Shop:

Do you run a Union Shop, if so this can be either a plus or a minus to your business? There are millions of union members in the USA and they have a tendency to support their fellow union brothers, but there are also millions of Americans that have been 'told' that all the nation's problems can be cured by getting rid of the unions. So, it is your decision as to whether you advertise your business as a union shop.

Many people believe that a union person provides better-educated and experienced contractors, but also believe that the cost will be more than the non-union enterprises. Many industrial and commercial clients will only use union shop contractors, others will not.

Warranty:

Do you warrant your work, your materials, your *start and completion time*, your qualifications, etc.? If so, and you should, then it will benefit you to have a *written warranty* and to either publish this on your website or at a minimum publish that a written copy of the warranty is available to those interested in hiring you or your firm.

Website Address:

Include your website address on all your *business card, flyers*, and *advertisements*. Also, if you are doing web pages that a client may copy, for instance some *educational content*, then put your website address at the bottom of the page so it will print out, and therefore be a reference for further exploration.

Website Name:

The website name is normally the *Domain Name*, and you must have a name that is unique to the world. John Smith Contracting is probably not unique and someone may have the name, which means you cannot. You have to do your homework and generate a listing of potential names for your company or website, and then test the Internet for the presence of the name. There are hundreds of website Internet service providers and most will have a means for you to see if your chosen name is unique among the millions of Internet names worldwide.

Caution, be ready to purchase the Domain Name the instant you find one that is not taken and suits your needs. There are people and companies that monitor Domain Name searches and when they see that you are interested in a name will immediately buy it, and then try to sell it to you at a very marked up price. Domain Names should not cost more than $10.00 per year, and these 'enterprising individuals' will attempt to sell you these $10 names at fees up to thousands of dollars.

Who Wrote the Internet Site:

It has become customary to put the name of the Webmaster on the footer of the website pages.

Workman's Compensation:

Do you have *family members working for you*? If so be careful, most will not be covered by Workman's Compensation if not specifically being paid by the company and thus, paying income taxes, federal and state taxes, and unemployment and worker's compensation taxes. This to a knowledgeable client can be a minus, and many will not hire you in the fear of having you or your relative suing their *homeowner's insurance* in the event of an accident. Thus, if you do provide Workman's Compensation and other worker benefits, it should be noted in your advertisements and on your Internet website.

Write a Review - Rate Service:

Having a 'Comment' page can provide great feedback as to how your clients feel about your work and job completions. Be aware that some people will use the comment page to complain about you. You can ignore these complaints, or you can answer each and attempt to make the client happy. Some of your readers will respect that, some will not and it may trigger more negative comments. I do NOT recommend you have a comment or Client Review page, but instead an email address where the client can send his or her complaint, and where you not only can answer in private, but resell that client on your product or services.

Confidence in Self and Products

Study the Competition

One of the primary things you should do, whether you are new to the area or been in business there for decades is to routinely study your *competition* and what it is doing. To not do this may allow them, the competition to advance ahead of you and therefore, cut into your current and future customer base.

Where Do They Advertise?

Start with looking at where the competition is advertising, is it where you are or have they found a new source of customers? Did they find a less expensive, but more effective way of advertising? Does their advertising appear to be working; have you studied it for a few months to see if they are continuing to advertise as they are?

What Are Their Shortcomings?

What are their shortcomings is it pricing, delivery, missed on-time appointments or schedules? Are they using out-of-date products and old technologies? Are they starting to appear worn and tired out and are they losing that fresh new guy look?

What Are Their Strengths?

What are their strengths, have they purchased new equipment, have they expanded into something new, or have they hired more experienced people?

You have to look at every competitor and keep a diary and charts on how you perceive that they are doing in comparison to you and your business. Then you have to see if you can do better at less cost and higher quality. If you do, then you should advertise that you do such and such, a plus for you and a minus for your competition.

Appearances:

Section on appearances, you, clothing, vehicles, personal looks, etc.

Contractor Etiquette:

Your Employees:

Do you have or are you going to hire helpers, if so you should make sure that each is a good representative of you and your contracting company. You need to set down a *code of conduct* and a *set of rules* as to what you expect from your people when he or she is on the job and with a client.

For example, I had a carpet installer in a building I was refurbishing and the installer brought with him a young helper. The older gentleman did excellent work, was very knowledgeable, and worked with precision and professional skills; the helper laid on the floor and bitched about how 'hard' life was, how difficult the work was, and he goofed off every time the older worker was out of his line of sight. The company that hired both men frankly cost themselves future jobs from me, as I will not tolerate this type of disrespect to me, the person paying for 'both' men's salary.

Training Your Personal to Be Salespeople:

You must also train your employees on how to be good salespeople; the person may be a carpet installer and laying down a Shag, but he or she can be looking at the remaining rooms and recommending other carpeting or flooring to the client. By assuring that he or she knows 'sales' techniques you increase the chances that you will get more work from the client, that day or in the future.

Also, there may be others 'viewing' the work being done, and they too may have a need for your services. Your employee can hand out your *business card* or *flyer*, but would it not be better to not have to wait for the potential client to call you, but to *ask for the sales appointment* right there and then, and then make the sale.

Offering Commissions:

People like to do things, first is to make money, the second is to belong to something, and by offering your salaried employees a 'sales' bonus or commission you fulfill both needs. You have trained your employees to recognize a potential sale, and taught him or her how to sell the sales appointment or item. They now feel that they helped you and did more than their 'normal' job requirement, thus by offering a commission you show that you 'appreciate' their extra effort and that you all are working as a team.

Your Brochure and Pricing Guide:

Updated Pricing Guide:

There are *Construction Estimating books* available that tend to standardize the cost and selling *prices of materials and labor* for just about any type of construction project. These guides are a handy starting point for your pricing, but you should always make decisions based on your experience of *man-hours*, problems that develop, materials, taxes, fees, profits, and such.

If you do the same basic work over and over for one or more clients, then you can develop a pricing guide that is unique to your business. This guide can be made available to your clients, if you wish, but if so then make sure that the guide is dated as being effective from date 'A' to date 'B'.

The drawback to having a public pricing guide is that your competition may obtain a copy and thus, try to undercut your pricing.

Product Photos and Selling Points:

I have seen many advertisements that include beautiful *color pictures or photographs* of the work that the contractor has completed for one or more of his or her clients, and for the most part this is good advertising. The objection is that the style shown may be to the client and some others great, while it may be not so great to others or me.

Additionally, I have a habit of looking at things and picking each apart, 'how does that work', and if I see your *mistakes*, then I will have some fun with you. Thus, if you are going to 'show off' your workmanship, be sure the picture is of something most will enjoy looking at and be sure there are no errors.

Professional Contract:

Your written contract, (You do have a *contract* do you not?), should be professionally developed and checked by an *attorney* for *loopholes* and problem areas. Many beginning construction contractors purchase ready made *'boilerplate'* or off-the-shelf contracts at a stationery store and use these. But, as you grow your business you may want to add a business name, logo, color, and other items to your printed contract.

You can also add some advertising so that when your client looks at the contract a year or two later (usually once it is paid or after taxes are over), he or she will see your advertisement and may again contract for your services.

Sales Calls:

Section is on making sales calls that fall into several different categories. There are Cold Calls, Response Calls, Recommendation Calls, and Callback Calls.

Your Market and Clients:

Target Market:

This is one of the first things you should attempt to isolate whenever you decide to offer products or services. It does not pay to offer 'Stair lifts to a market of which 99% of the buyers are athletes. Your markets are those who are aging or injured and need help staying in their two and three story homes.

Who Is The Buyer:

You go to a person's home and you talk to the husband for an hour about adding on the extra room. You measure, prepare the paperwork, do the estimate, and hand him a pen and the contract, only to find out he is renting and you have to deal with the landlord. What just happened, you failed to qualify the person that has the authorization to actually make the purchase.

Interpreters and Translators - Languages

You get a call to come to such and such address and quote new carpet. You get there and find that the only person there, the owner, is Korean and only speaks Korean, which you do not. This is getting more common as the nation becomes more diversified and is accepting foreign nations into our schools, colleges, companies, and communities.

So what to do? You can purchase pocket-sized translator computers for under a $100 these days, and these machines will allow you to speak your language and have it almost instantly translated, and the client can speak his or her language and have it instantly translated. Or you can knock on doors and hope to find a neighbor the can speak both languages and is willing to help you make the sale.

Practice Your Sales Pitch:

Believe it or not, many salespeople have not a clue as to what they are selling. They did not take the time to study and learn the product. Also, many get nervous when meeting a new potential client and therefore, botch the introduction or sale's pitch.

I suggest that not only do you study every aspect of the product or service you are offering, but you also practice, practice, practice, your sale's pitch and your answers to as many possible questions a potential client may ask. Do this in front of a mirror to watch your reflection and mannerisms that you project, then in front of a neighbor, co-worker, or other person that can be trusted to 'tell you the truth'. If necessary, hire a few high school or college kids, or a few seniors. They will listen and give you reasonably good feedback as to your presentation and if it is understandable to a person that is NOT familiar with the product or service being offered. (Reason, family will lie to you, and a co-worker may understand the technical aspects, but a stranger may not).

Educate Your Client:

Don't be afraid to educate your client on the benefits of your product or service. Just do not make the person feel 'stupid' by going to far. Example: I had a teacher that was teaching Residential Electrical Wiring; he stood in front of the class holding up a piece of wire and repeated over a dozen times, "this is a wire, this is a wire,..."

Listening to The Client:

This is one of the most important things you can do; listen to your client. Yep, you are the expert and if the client says something you just have to 'jump in' and put in your two-cents. This is a sure way to lose the sale for several reasons: First is that you are 'rude' for interrupting and that is a strike against you. Second is that you failed to hear everything the client was about to say, which could have been "Where do I Sign?" Third is that you are missing the indicators that tell you exactly what the client wants and thus, you have no way of answering his or her needs or objections.

Evening and Weekend Appointments:

Working 9 to 5 Monday thru Friday is great, especially if you have so much business you are booked solid for several weeks to months. But if you are not, then you have to work to your client's schedules, after all they are the people that will be or are paying your wages. This frequently will mean that you have to work evenings and weekends due to the clients working 9 to 5 Monday thru Friday.

Get Their EMail Address:

People get phone calls by the hundreds during the week, many of these calls are scams or junk sale's calls and therefore are not answered or put on the 'do not call list'. Thus, you need a way to contact these clients that has a good chance of being read, and that is email. Be sure to put your name or company name in the Subject Line, along with a short description of the email contents.

Ask for the JOB:

You would be surprised at how many will not ask for the job.

Drive By:

Are you a painting contractor, if so do you drive the local neighborhood and look at the stores, factories, residential homes, etc.? You should, for there are 'leads' just staring you in the face; the faded paint, chipping and peeling paint, new construction, etc. Don't be afraid to stop and 'ask', present yourself and your business card or flyer directly to the owner or resident. Let them know you are a neighborhood contractor and not a 'fly-by-night'.

Construction Sites:

Most construction sites have already hired the workers that are on the site and doing the job or will be. You need to let the 'Contractor' firm know that you have skills that they may need, and that you are available.

Visit Other Contractors:

You may be a painter, but not a plumber or electrician. Get to know these people as they during their work see the inside of homes and businesses and therefore have first-hand knowledge of those that may need your services. You recommend them, and they you; good for both businesses, providing each are good contractors and do a good job for their clients.

If you are a jerk, or they, then the recommendations can be a negative to one or both.

Join Union Contractors In The Area:

Your area may have carpenters, plumbers, and electricians that are in a local or national union. If you decide to join their union you will get the benefits of access to jobs, access to better pay, access to health care plans, and access to legal if ever required.

The downside is that you have to start at the bottom, as an apprentice to a senior member of the trade in which you are working. It can take years until you have the necessary apprentice experience and can pass the test for Journeyman, and then two or more years until you become a 'Master' contractor.

Keep Your Eyes And Ears Open:

Going to a bar, a party, church, school, or some event? Keep your eyes and ears open to the conversations around you, you may just find that a person is telling his or her friend about a need, a job that was botched, or some other item that can produce a lead for you and your next job.

Not a Gypsy:

During periods of the year, usually seasonal, there are those that travel from area to area selling their services. These people are considered to be Gypsies and although some are legitimate, many are not. Gypsies tend to travel with the weather by heading to northern states in the spring and summer, and to the southern states in the fall and winter. They sell all sorts of contracting services, and may ask for large up-front money claiming they need to purchase the supplies for your job.

They usually work an area for a week or two, taking deposits, and then either do sub-quality work or non at all before they move on to another area.

You need to let your clients know that you are 'permanent' to the area in which you service, and that you will be there for them if any problems arise.

As for deposits, the laws usually allow for a 10% up-front deposit at the signing of the contract, and then one or more 'performance' payments over the length of the contract equal 80% of the contracted price, and then finally the last 10% when the client signs off that he or she is satisfied with the work and cleanup.

Subcontracting:

Are you willing to be a subcontractor to others? The flooring industry is famous for this, the selling company does little to none of the installation of the flooring, and they subcontract the jobs to private contractors that they trust. If you are not comfortable with talking to clients, doing and tracking advertising, and worrying about when your next sale is coming, then perhaps being a subcontractor to a 'sales' organization is a better career move for you.

Overcoming Objections:

"Do you have it in blue?" "Yes I do!" "Do you have it in Green?" "Yes I do!" "How about in Red?" See where this is going, it is going to end up with the client asking if you have it in 'Nutty-Fruity-Orange' or some other color you do not have.

Let's start over. "Do you have it in blue?" "Do you want it if I do?" The client now has to answer either "Yes" or "No". If he or she answers "Yes" then you hand them the contract and a pen. If he or she answers "No", then you ask, "What Color do you want?" They now have to tell you, and you now hand them the contract and a pen. (I am assuming you have that color)

Let's say you spent the good part of an hour with a client trying to make the sale and you have gotten nowhere. What to do? You can just pack up and thank the person for his or her time and then leave, or you can look defeated, pack up like you are leaving, and walk to the door. STOP there! Now turn and ask, "What exactly did I do wrong, did I insult you? Did I give you bad information? Etc. make it personal so that they have to answer. Most will never say that you insulted them or gave them bad information and their answer to your questions will be "No".

So now you have a chance to again ask, "So, what was it that you did not like about the estimate or presentation?" Now they are forced to answer with the real reason that they have objected to closing the sale with you. Let's say that their answer is "Well, I believe you are using inferior materials and I don't like that". Your response is, "So, the only (make sure you use the word ONLY) reason you are not purchasing from me is that you believe I am using inferior materials, is that correct?" Again you have put the client in a situation where he or she has to answer "Yes" or "No".

If the answer is "Yes", then come back with "So, since that is your only objection, will you purchase if I provide materials that are suitable to you?" If the answer is "NO", then you come back with "So that is not your only objection, what else did you not like?".

The reason for this is simple. The person called you for an estimate, and thus he or she is ready to purchase; and you are there to sell him or her the item or service. All you have to do is find out what he or she really expects and then let him or her know you CAN provide it.

Silence is Golden:

I was trying to sell a potential buyer a room full of carpet; I did the measurements, presented the samples, and we selected the color, brand, and quality. I then wrote up the estimate and handed it across the table to the client for his signature. He did not sign. I had a choice, ask why he was not signing or just sit there in silence. If I asked why, he would have presented me with one thing after another and it may take hours if at all to make the sale. I chose to just sit and remain silent. We sat there looking at each other for 45 minutes, he finally reached over and took my $10.00 calculator and a pen and signed the contract for $2,500 worth of carpet. All he wanted was to 'win' something, anything.

Increasing Sales:

Buyer Remorse:

Buyer remorse is a psychological effect that frequently happens when a client 'thinks' that he or she made the wrong decision by hiring you. This could be that he or she found a better price after the job was contracted, or that he or she did not like the color, placement, quality, etc. of the items you supplied.

One way to attempt to protect yourself from Buyer Remorse is to complement the client on his or her selection of color, placement, quality etc. thus letting them know that they are 'smart' and did the right thing.

Example: "Well I am finished, and frankly I had my doubts when I started this job, but sir (or Madam) your selection and ideas are really impressive".

Paperwork and Warranty Ads:

If your contracting is for items that require state or local permits, then be sure to include in your advertising that you provide all permits, licensing, bonding, and such in your contracts. You may also by law have to post your license number in all ads.

Government Rebates:

Some governments, usually local or state, may offer rebates if you purchase 'Green Energy' type products, or you add Solar to your home, or replace windows etc. and most contractors know about these rebates.

Unfortunately, some contractors will not inform their clients of the rebate and keep it for themselves. This adds to their bottom-line profits and on the surface looks good for them.

Ask yourself, if you do a job for a client and you keep the rebate money without telling him or her, and he or she finds out that you did, do you think you will get a positive 'word of mouth' recommendation?

Selling Upscale:
Talk to your potential clients and listen to their answers. Why are they considering your services? How long are they planning on living or staying in the building? Are they preparing for a pending sale of the property? The reason for finding these things is that if a client is going to continue to occupy the property for years or decades, then it may pay him or her to upgrade to better materials. For example, a 25-year roof shingle instead of a 20-year shingle that may actually wear out in 15.

Follow Up Sales:
When a person contracts for a service or product he or she may have carefully budgeted for the item, and thus can only afford that item. You are selected as the contractor and you do a good job, but see that other items need your services. Talk to the client about this and why he or she is not getting the other items taken care of at this time. This opens the door to future work as you now may be able to present the client with alternative financing and close the deal before leaving that day, or you can find out the client's timetable and potential future budget. This allows you to send the client a 'reminder' when the appropriate time arrives.

Maintenance Contracts:
See Add-ons below.

Maintenance Reminder Cards or Letters:

Appliances and other items like the Air Conditioner or the Water Heater require periodic preventive maintenance. Most owners do not consider this maintenance as the item is working and thus, out of sight out of mind.

You send them a 'maintenance reminder' per the manufacturer's schedule and you have opened the door to selling a service call. You are also keeping your name in front of that client that already knows that you did good work for him or her in the past. Thus, there is a good chance that they will recommend you to their friends and if needed, hire you again.

Coupons:

Business a little slow, then perhaps you need to 'spike' your normal advertising with a coupon or 'special offer'. These are to be done no more than one or two times a year. Some companies have 'sales' every two days or so, and thus potential clients consider these as con's or 'leader items' that come with a 'hitch' or unreasonable condition.

If you do present a coupon, then be sure to have the conditions spelled out, and the dates the coupon if valid displayed. Don't forget your company name and contact information, and any other information that the client needs to know.

Add-ons:

I love it when a company sells me an item and then immediately tries to sell me an extended warranty. If the product is good, then why do I need to purchase a warranty? Shouldn't the product last for more than 90 days or a year?

What you can sell as an 'add-on' is a preventive maintenance contract as everyone knows that 'things' need periodic maintenance and that by performing that maintenance the product will last much longer and cost less in the long run.

You can also sell things like a cleaning each season, or a Winterization. For example, you did a repair on a person's pool pump and now you offer to clean the pool in the spring for the summer opening, and winterize it in the fall for the winter closing. Sell, Sell, and Sell.

Selling Safety:

Selling Safety is relatively easy as most clients want to be safe, they do not want to be electrocuted, have a beam fall on their head, or have a gas line explode. The key to selling safety is to NOT oversell it to the point that the client thinks you are 'Bs'ing' him or her.

You can do things like, "Sir, I noticed that your bathroom electrical outlets do not seem to be GFI protected. If you plan on selling in the future you may have to have these installed. GFI is a requirement these days and it can protect you or your love ones from getting shocked."

Selling Experience:

If you have the experience to do the job for which you are bidding, then by all means let your potential client know that you have successfully done this type of work before.

Selling Price:

This is something you probably should not do as the price you quote may be too low or too high, and may not be in line with your competitor's pricing. It is better to sell the job, and then after the client sees that you know what you are doing, that you are providing the better material and workmanship, you talk price.

The reason is this. The potential client may have already had one or more bids from competitors, and if your bid is out of line with their, the client will just dismiss you without knowing anything about how you work or what kinds of materials, warrantees, time schedules, etc. you can provide.

Selling Clean Up:

I ran a successful consumer electronics repair facility for several years and learned a 'trick'. My competitor would take in a machine for repair and do a fine job at a decent cost. He would also just give the machine back to the customer in the same condition as he received it, usually with fingerprints, dirt, food, and other contaminants on the surfaces.

I instructed my employees to spend an extra 5-minutes and clean and polish each machine when the repair was completed. The units were then wrapped in new plastic and presented in like new condition to the client. The clients went out of their way to recommend my shop, as they knew I cared about their investment, and them.

Selling License and Permits and Inspections:

There are all sorts of 'contractors' out there in the world and most are reasonably good at what they do, and I have to admit that being licensed by the state does NOT always mean good quality work. But, the fact that a person or company is licensed, and therefore is subject to state laws does make one feel more secure.

So, if you are licensed, and you are following the laws and building codes, then be sure to let your potential clients know this fact. Let them know that you will be, if necessary, having delays while portions of the job are being inspected by the state employees, and that you may have to secure blueprints, material listings, and such; and that these not only cost money, but will aid in the future if the home or building is to be sold.

Unauthorized work can and probably will cause problems if the client tries to sell the property, and can result in costly redoes, and possibly fines.

Selling Hauling Cleanup:

You are bidding on replacing an old fence for a client and the deal is just within inches of being complete, but the client is balking and will not sign the contract, so what do you do? You pull out your 'Ace' card, you say something like this; *"Mr. (name) I realize that you really want the fencing that I am supplying and probably need some time to make your decision, but I tell you what, will you sign the contract if I agree to haul away the old fence material for you?"* The chances are that he will sign the contract; after all you just saved him some work, time, and possible expense.

Puppy Dog Selling:

61

This is a trick from decades ago that still works today; how do you sell a puppy dog? The answer is to give the puppy to the customer for a week and then come back and try to take it away; the chances are that you will not be able to get the puppy back, the new owners will gladly pay your price. This also worked in the 1950's when television started to become popular, the dealer would give you a two week 'trial' period and then come and pick up the set, or try to.

So, if you have an item that can be 'loaned' for a week or two, you have a way of selling it.

Brand Name Recognition

This is the psychological aspect of a sale. You let your client know that you use 'brand name' products instead of the 'no-name' products that may not be as superior. Frankly, there are many unknown products that work very well, but to a client that is paying for quality, he or she will appreciate the 'brand name item' and question the no-name item.

Provide Financing:

If you can, then provide your client with an alternative to 'cash' as many people just do not have the cash to spend even if the need is critical, i.e. the A/C just stopped working during a heat wave.

Killing a Sale:

Overselling:

You have presented the sales pitch to the client and now you *'shut up'* and wait for the potential customer to say something, but the seconds tic by and you get nervous and open your mouth and start selling again.

This is a form of overselling and it only opens up the client to doubts and more objections and questions that you have to now answer. Your job is to sell the job, and once you have made the sales pitch you should 'shut up' and see what happens, even if you have to sit there for an hour in dead silence. Eventually, the potential client will say something, and that is 'ok, we got a deal' or 'here is my objection', and either way you win, you have a way to 'close' the sale and make some money.

Another oversell is to *panic* when you feel that the potential client is not interested and therefore, you start to offer 'extras' that are not in your original estimate. These extras will usually cost you time and money, but more importantly you have now signaled to the potential client that you are willing to give '*extras*'; and as a savvy client he or she will now go for the gold and try to get more and more 'extras' out of you for the original price quoted. Thus, the suggestion is to make your sales presentation, put the contract in front of the potential client, and then 'shut up'. He or she will tell you how to proceed.

Overselling in your advertisements; we have a flooring company in Philadelphia that states that they will 'give' you three free rooms of flooring when you purchase one room of carpeting at their regular price. This may get some uninformed potential clients to bite and invite the salesperson to his or her home, but most potential clients understand that you do not get three rooms of free flooring, the price is included in the price of the one room or the quality of the flooring for the remaining rooms is substandard, or both.

Sounds Too Good:
'If it sounds too good to be true, beware' is the warning given to consumers by most *consumer protection organizations* and by our governments, thus be careful with your advertisements and sales pitches, for if it does sound too good to be true, the potential customer may avoid your service or product.

Example: We can build you a full kitchen for only $1,500 would be an advertisement that will catch the eye, but cannot be. What are you providing and what are you leaving out at that price would be the question of any potential customer that has ever been to a home builder's supply. The cabinets alone will usually cost $2,500 or more, and when you add in flooring, painting, appliances, permits, etc. the $1,500 price appears to be false advertising, and therefore the majority of potential clients will pass.

Promises Not Kept:

"Yes, Mrs. Jones we will be there at 8 am on Tuesday." You *fail to show* at 8 am and therefore, you have 'ticked off' this client. People really do not usually care as to when you can start a job, most understand that you are busy and you must schedule multiple jobs, therefore if you try to sell a job by making a promise of being there on Tuesday when you know you can never make it, you are setting yourself up for problems. Even if the client lets you in on Wednesday a day late, he or she will 'suspect' all of your work and you may be spending most of your time overcoming objections to this and that.

People make plans, and if you say you are going to be there at 8 am on Tuesday, the client plans for this and may have changed his or her schedule, or missed a day of work, or postponed another appointment, etc. and therefore when you do not show, you are harming him or her.

This is the same for all promises made, including what products you are using, what you are going to do, the types of financing offered, etc. If you make a promise, then keep it, or lose not only this client, but also all the other potential clients this person knows.

False Advertising:
It is reasonable to try and make yourself or your company look better than it actually is, but there is a limit on this, and that limit is to provide totally false or untrue information in your sales pitch or advertising.

You may get away with this for a period and you may make a few extra dollars, but as soon as the word gets around that you are a cheat, you will find yourself out of business, which is contrary to what you intended. So, the tip of the day is 'don't do it', leave out the *'We are number one'* stuff, as it can be easily shown that you are not, there is always someone better; and there will always be a competitor that can prove you falsely advertised, and if done with the *intent to defraud*, you can end up fined or in jail.

Selling Fear:
Selling fear is not a bad thing, providing you do it in a way that results in the client thanking you for 'protecting' him or her from potential harm. *For example*; Telling a client that unless the garage has a two

64

hour fire wall, it could be dangerous to the client's family is ok, whereas telling the client that God will certainly punish him or her if they do not install a two hour firewall in the garage is not productive.

Life and Health and other insurance agencies use fear all the time for selling to a client, and it is very effective. But to try to sell fear to a person who wants a new kitchen floor is going a little overboard, and many potential customers will realize this and consider you a flake and then dismiss you without partaking of your services.

Mispricing The Job:

This is very common in that you are *'guesstimating'* the *cost of the job* based on your research of labor of materials or your past experience, but you now find that this job is somewhat more difficult and will take more time and money to complete, so what do you do?

Many beginning contractors will either take *shortcuts* to make up for the losses, or will attempt to get more money from the client, or will just quit the job and walk, all things that are sure to get your reputation spread in the community within minutes.

If you *underestimate a job* and you do not have a written contract that specifies that 'unforeseen' items that develop can result in increased time, materials, and cost, then just be silent and eat difference, take the loss and chalk it up to experience. To do otherwise is to ask for a bad reference and a loss of reputation and future clients.

Failure To Appear:

Failing to appear at the job at the day and time that was specified will certainly lose you a customer, even if you have a good excuse. The customer has relied on your promise to be at their place at a certain date and time and therefore, may have changed their daily schedule to accommodate your arrival and working time for the job. This may have cost this person time, accrued holiday or vacation hours, and lost wages, and therefore he or she will not be happy.

Now, if you find that you absolutely have to *miss an appointment*, then call and speak to the client and explain the reason or circumstances, items like you were in a car accident or your wife is having a baby are generally overlooked, providing it is true. If it is not true and you lie about the reason for not making the appointment, and the client finds out, then you can probably kiss goodbye that client and all of his or her relatives, friends, and coworkers as potential customers. *Word of mouth*, again will prevail.

Even if you do not miss the appointment, but are *late* you can be in trouble, thus make sure you schedule appointments with enough time allowance to complete each and get to the next on time.

Making Major Errors:

Every contractor will at one time have a major 'boo boo' day; something will go horribly wrong and you will have to face the customer and try to explain the problem encountered, this is normal business. What is not normal is to try to cover up the major mistake or to try and blame it on the customer or to lie about what actually happened. These *'cover your butt' type fixes* will almost always come back to bite you, so don't do it. Admit to the client that you made an error, explain the procedure you will use to fix the problem, and eat the labor and materials cost, that is good business, and good business is good advertising.

Bad Mouthing The Competition:

Here is one of the easiest ways to lose a client; you badmouth the competition in your attempt to make yourself look better. It is perfectly fine to point out that you do this and that some competitors in general do not, but to name a specific competitor is not conducive to good business.

Here are a few reasons: One the competitor turns out to be the brother-in-law of your potential customer. Two, the competition finds out about your statements and can prove in court that you were wrong and libeled him or her. Three, the client may have used the competitor before and was satisfied, and is only using you because the competitor was too busy to do the job at hand in the allotted time. Either way, you have made a fool of yourself and probably lost a client for life.

Contractor's Opportunities:

We in the USA have been provided with one of the best opportunities since the great depression of 1929, the opportunity to rebuild the country and its neglected and failing infrastructure.

We have an opportunity to build using materials and products manufactured here, in America, by Americans who will be paying into the tax base for generations to come.

A small business, like your local contractor, does not stop advertising when things get bad, he or she increases the spending and looks for ways to increase revenue, usually by purchasing better equipment and tools and sending his or her employees to schools. You work your way out of a Depression or Recession, you do NOT cut spending that only puts more people out of work, cuts more educational opportunities for future improvement, and forces an already hurting business out of business.

With this said:

Opportunity # 1 - The Fire Department:
Get to know a few of the local firefighters, they know of the kitchen fires, the warehouse that burned, the house where the owner burned up his or her bed or carpet with careless smoking, etc. These are all 'leads' that if you offer services like fire and smoke restoration, carpet replacements, carpentry, dry walling, texture coating, painting, wiring, plumbing, etc. you have an 'in' and an opportunity.

Opportunity # 2 - HUD
There are tens of thousands of HUD (Housing and Urban Development) homes on the market due to the economic downturn, and most of these homes are vacant which leads to unscrupulous peoples stripping wiring, plumbing, appliances, etc. from the buildings. HUD by law has to offer these homes to low income people for a period, and then can take investor bids. You need to follow these HUD properties carefully as many times safety repairs have to be made before the homes are sold; at other times the new owners will need your services restoring the damages; and at other times you yourself may qualify for the home at a substantially reduced price from market; thus the opportunity for making profits exist on three or more levels.

Opportunity # 3 - Travel

Are you willing to travel to other states or countries? There are opportunities for construction contractors in all states and most countries; you just have to seek out these opportunities. Look at what is happening throughout the South and Midwestern states with the weather; draughts, fires, floods, tornadoes, hurricanes, ice storms, and heat waves have destroyed fences, walls, foundations, homes, businesses, factories, HVAC systems, electrical systems, water wells and systems, glass, roofs, pools, etc. by the tens of thousands. You may need permission to operate in 'declared emergency' zones, but after a period all are invited as the locals are usually overwhelmed with work and are looking for your service as a contractor or subcontractor.

Opportunity # 4 - People are Broke

How is this an opportunity, well if a person is looking at his or her water, gas, and electric bills and wondering why he or she is paying nearly twenty-five percent of his or her pay to the Utility companies, he or she may start looking for a better way.

This usually means an Energy Audit or more insulation, heater or air conditioner replacements, newer energy efficient doors and windows, carpets over the hardwood, new insulated curtains and blinds, better and lower cost lighting, automatic energy monitoring and controllers, and new appliances. People will spend money to save money over the long haul.

Opportunity # 5 - Real Estate MLS

Most all towns have a Real Estate office and that office has homes and businesses listed on the MLS (Multiple Listing Service). Many of these REs (Real Estates) will show you how to access the MLS via the Internet where you can see what is being offered for sale and what has been sold recently. Each home or business being sold usually needs work; work to put it in compliance with local and federal laws, work to improve the salability of the property, and work after the sale to bring the place up to the expectations of the new owners.

Opportunity # 6 - Dead People

When a person dies, he or she usually leaves behind property and kinfolk, and this usually means that there is a ton of cleanup to be done, and a ton of work getting the property ready for the market. Once sold there is work for the new owners.

Opportunity # 7 - Renters

Lots of unsuspecting people purchase duplexes and other small apartment buildings expecting to make a profit or at least have a constant income. The actual results are usually tenants that destroy half the place or leave it smelling like the town dump. Yes, there are good tenants that do take care of the property as if it is theirs, but in those instances where the tenant did not care, you have an opportunity to help the owner quickly bring the space back to a livable and rentable condition.

Opportunity # 8 - Senior Clubs

As a person grows older he or she can no longer do the chores that he or she once did; this is due to one's health, getting weaker with age, losing ones hearing or sight, and a host of other problems. For the contractor, this becomes an opportunity to lower kitchen cabinets, add safety railings at doorways, on stairs, and in the bath, provide better lighting, better security, and better means of communication devices. Learn what the elderly need and you can make good money supplying to those needs.

Contact and visit a few local area Senior Clubs, set up 30 to 45 minute seminars with the Senior Clubs, you will have a captive audience. As you prove yourself you will become more and more in demand, but a word of caution, do not 'screw' a Senior with poor quality, poor service, high prices, etc. as their network is wide and they can 'ruin' your reputation within seconds.

Opportunity # 9 - Stores

Most food stores require good lighting, good security systems, and good refrigeration systems and most contract for the installation and maintenance of these systems. Watch for vacant stores, newly rented stores, etc. there is usually work that needs to be done to bring the store up to codes, and to make it as the owner believes it should be.

Appendix I - Contractor and Construction Organizations:

Air Conditioning Contractors Association ACCA
American Institute of Architects (AIA)
American National Standards Institute (ANSI)
American Pipeline Contractors Association (APCA)
American Society of Heating, Refrigerating and Air-Conditioning Engineers (ASHRAE)
American Society of Testing and Materials (ASTM)
American Solar Energy Society (ASES)
Associated Builders & Contractors (ABC)
Associated General Contractors of America. (AGC)
Associated Master Painters and Decorators of Philadelphia (AMPD).
Association of the Wall and Ceiling Industry (AWCI)
Association of Women Contractors (AWC)

Better Business Bureau (BBB)
Brick Industry Association (BIA)
Building Officials and Code Administrators (BOCA)
Building Service Contractors Association International (BSCAI)

California Building Performance Contractors Association or (CBPCA)
California Landscape Contractors Association ... (CLCA)
Ceramic Tile Institute of America (CTIOA)
Colorado Contractors Association (CCA)

Firestop Contractors International Association (FCIA)

General Builders and Contractors Association (GBCA)

Illinois Land Improvement Contractors Association (ILICA)
Independent Electrical Contractor Association - (IECI)
Institute for Research In Construction (IRC) - Canada
Institute of Electrical and Electronics Engineers (IEEE)
International Association of Drilling Contractors (IADC)
International Association of Plumbing and Mechanical Officials (IAPMO)
International Door Association (IDA)

International Masonry Institute (IMI)
International Solar Energy Society (ISES)

Land Improvement Contractors Association LICA

Maryland Minority Contractors Association. MMCA
Mason Contractors Association of America (MCAA)
Master Plumbers Association of Wisconsin (MPA)
Mechanical Contractors Association of America (MCAA)
Mechanical Contractors Association. (MCA)
Minority Business Enterprise / Women's Business Enterprise
(MBE/WBE)

National Asphalt Pavement Association - NAPA
National Association of Minority Contractors (NAMC)
National Association of Plumbing-Heating-Cooling Contractors
(PHCC)
National Black Contractors Association's (BBCA)
National Demolition Association (NDA)
National Electrical Contractors Association (NECA)
National Fire Protection Association (NFPA)
National Independent Contractors Association (NICA)
National Roofing Contractors Association (NRCA)
National Utility Contractors Association NUCA
Native American Contractors Association (NACA)

Occupational Safety and Health Administrator. (OSHA)

Painting & Decorating Contractors of America (PDCA)
Plumbing-Heating-Cooling Contractors Association (PHCC)

Renovation, Repair and Painting Program, (RRP)
Roofing Contractors Association of California (RCAC)

Sheet Metal and Air Conditioning Contractors National Association
(SMACNA) -
Slate Roofing Contractor's Association (SRCA).
Solar Electric Power Association (SEPA)
Solar Energy Industries Association (SEIA)

Southwest Washington Contractors Association (SWCA)

Timber Framers Guild of North America American Window and Door Institute (AWDI).

Western States Roofing Contractors Association - (WSRCA)
Wood Flooring Contractor's Association (WFCA)

Appendix II - Building Codes

A National Resource for Global Standards (NSSN)
Accessible and Usable Buildings and Facilities (ANSI A117.1)
American Standard National Plumbing Code
Americans with Disabilities Act Accessibility Guidelines (ADAAG)

Canadian National Building Code (CNBC)

International Code Council (ICC)
International Mechanical Code (IMC)
International Plumbing Code (IPC)

Life Safety Code (NFPA 101)

Model Energy Code (MEC)

National Association of Steel Framed Housing (NASH)
National Building Code (NBC)
National Electrical Code (NEC),
National Electrical Safety Code (NESC)
National Energy Conservation Code (NECC)
National Fire Codes and Standards, Volumes 1-12 (NFPA)
National Fire Codes® Subscription Service (NFCSS)
National Fire Prevention Code (NFPC)
National Fuel Gas Code(NFPA 54)
National Insulation Association's (NIA)
National Lighting Code (NLC)
National Mechanical Code (NMC)
National Plumbing Code (NPC)
National Property Maintenance Code (NPMC)
National Standard Plumbing Code (NSPC)

Standard Gas Code (SGC)
Standard Mechanical Code (SMC)
Standard Plumbing Code (SPC)
Standard Building Code (SBC)
Standard Fire Prevention Code (SFPC)

Uniform Building Code (UBC)
Uniform Fire Code (UFC)
Uniform Mechanical Code (UMC)
Uniform Plumbing Code (UPC)
Uniform Sign Code (USC)

Appendix III - Advertising Page Sizes

Sample ad sizes

Center Spread 21.25" wide x12.25" deep
Full Page 10.25" wide x 12.25" deep
4/5 Page (vertical) 8.17" wide x 12.25" deep
4/5 Page (horizontal) 10.25" wide x 10" deep
Jumbo Jr. Page 8.17" wide x 10.7" deep
Jr. Page 8.17" wide x 10" deep
3/5 Page 6.08" wide x 12.25" deep
1/2 Page (vertical) 5" wide x 12.25" deep
1/2 Page (horizontal) 10.25" wide x 6.125" deep
2/5 Page 4" wide x 12.25" deep
3/10 Page 6.08" wide x 6.125" deep
1/5 Page (vertical) 1.9" wide x 12.25" deep
1/5 Page (horizontal) 4" wide x 6.125" deep
1/10 Page 1.9" wide x 6.125" deep

Sample Page / Column Sizes:

Page is 6 columns wide by 172 lines deep. Width of page is 10.125";
depth is 12.25". Borders or cuts permitted. Minimum size ad: 4 lines.
Minimum size display ad: 14 lines (14 agate lines equals 1 inch).

Column Widths 1 column 1.572" 2 columns 3.308" 3 columns 5.043"
4 columns 6.779" 5 columns 8.515" 6 columns 10.125"

Index:

Author:

The author in his prime was a building designer, contractor, and builder. He has designed Duplexes, Triplexes, and other buildings; as well as kitchens, baths, and storage building.

He has published construction books and articles for Prentice Hall, Craftsman Book Company, Family Handyman Magazine, and has served as an 'Expert Witness' in court case disputes.

His Construction Books Are:
Fences and Retaining Walls – Craftsman Book Company
Painter's Handbook – Craftsman Book Company
Electrical Blueprint Reading – Craftsman Book Company
Roof Builder's Handbook – Prentice Hall

His Travel Manuals are on Amazon.com/Kindle books.

Cover Picture:

Typical house job opportunities are Roofing, Painting, Windows,

Doors, Patio, Electrical, Plumbing, Sewer, Railings, Skylight, Stairs, Tree Cutting, Landscaping, Chimney Cleaning, and Driveway replacements and maintenance. Each of which is a 'Sales Opportunity' that can make you money.

www.ingramcontent.com/pod-product-compliance
Lightning Source LLC
Chambersburg PA
CBHW020607220526
45463CB00006B/2492